The Story of Bella

A Tale of Confidence, Trust, and Love

by Patricia Garza Pinto

Dedication

As Patricia, mother to Monica
and grandmother to Bella,
I dedicate this heartfelt book
as a tribute to
the resilience of children,
including that of my
beloved granddaughter, Bella.
I commend her for triumphing
over her childhood speech impediment,
and my gratitude flows to Monica
for nurturing such a resilient daughter.

This book is also dedicated to
the resilience of the inner child in You.
To those who battle shame and insecurity,
may you rediscover your
true strength and inner beauty.

Preface

In my earthly purpose to support
women facing life's challenges,
I share this book with
both children and adults,
to let you know that,
if you are willing to dig deep enough,
if you are willing to face yourself,
and
if you are willing to follow your heart,
you can overcome any obstacle
and manifest your dreams.

Once upon a time, in a small town filled with laughter and sunshine, lived a precious five year-old girl. Bella had soft, flowing chestnut-colored hair and big, bright blue eyes that sparkled with joy and love. She was a special girl, a crystal child with an inner knowing of her true essence. But, she felt a little different from the other children. You see, Bella had a speech impediment. She could not pronounce her "r's".

This caused some challenges for Bella. Some of the other children in preschool giggled and teased her when she spoke. Even her teacher scolded her for not being able to say her "r's". Bella felt ashamed and embarrassed, as though something was wrong with her.

The first time she was made to feel her difference happened on a bright sunny day while she was outside, playing on the monkey bars. Two children approached her and stood quietly staring. After they whispered in each other's ears, one of the girls walked closer to Bella and commanded,

"Say the word 'hair'!"

To her best ability, Bella replied,

"Hai."

Hearing this, the young girls laughed and pointed at her, then ran away to the swings.

Bella jumped off the monkey bars and ran to the corner of the playground, where she sat with her head on her arms and wiped the tears from her face.

Fortunately, Bella had a strong, unshakeable spirit with a heart bigger than her head, and she did not let the teasing make her feel small. She found comfort in the unconditional love of her dog, Revilo, and in her connection with nature. Together, they explored its wonders, running through the wildflower fields, chasing butterflies, and playing fetch with an old, tattered softball that Revilo had found in the street gutter.

She also loved to create things that reflected her soulful heart, and she painted the beauty she saw around her in bright colorful masterpieces. Her favorite painting was of Crescent Bay beach and the ocean where she loved to swim.

One day several years later, her friend invited her to a softball game, and it was there that Bella discovered her other passion. She watched the pitcher, captivated by her focus, power, and grace. In her bed that night, Bella dreamed of becoming a pitcher for the local girls' softball team. From that moment on, her hand spent hours perfecting its grip on the tattered, old softball, maneuvering it between her fingers. Over and over again, she practiced tossing the softball into the air and catching it. Fairly soon, Bella was ready to play on her city's softball league team.

Unfortunately, Bella was met with a few difficulties. She was taller than the other girls, and her long, slightly bowed legs made her appear awkward when she ran. Her artist's love of the beauty in nature distracted her focus from the game, and she could not help but dance with the flowers in the field. The creative free-spirit of her longed to connect with mother nature and the magical earth spirits, as she had done when she was a young child. The coaches always picked her last. Her speech impediment made it challenging to communicate with her teammates and coaches. Some of the players doubted her ability and did not take her seriously.

Bella didn't understand and often laid in bed at night crying. But, she never gave up. Bella had inherited her inner spirit of resilience from her mother, and she believed in herself. Refusing to roll over, she knew that she could overcome any obstacle. In proving her ability to play the game, she just needed commitment, focus, and hard work.

After practices, while some of the girls played on their cell phones or discussed the latest hair and fashion trends, Bella practiced her pitching. Standing on the green and white pitching mat, she pitched fastball after fastball into the orange and black net. During solo practice, Bella mixed up her pitches with change up, slow pitches.

Seeing her passion and determination, Bella's parents and grandparents sought out the help of a pitching coach and a batting coach to provide weekly lessons for her. Bella was diligent and followed the expert instruction of her experienced coaches, and her pitches became stronger, faster, more accurate, and more determined. She often imagined herself on the pitcher's mound of a professional softball stadium, surrounded by high bright spot lights and cheering fans, watching her throw the perfect underhand fast pitch.

Days turned into weeks, weeks into months, and months into years, until Bella's dedication and practice paid off. The day came when she was given the opportunity to pitch for her softball team in the annual state championship tournament games.

On game day, Bella and her teammates were tired from the previous games, but their spirits were high. Fueled by the support of families and friends, Bella felt a surge of confidence and strength rise from deep within her. She had come so far. She was finally doing what she had dreamt and desired, to pitch a championship softball game. Bella had proved herself to her team, and their trust in her was unwavering.

Despite the blistering rays of the sun, an overheated and sweaty Bella and her teammates prepared and practiced. After each pitch, ball, walk, and strike out, Bella wiped the sweat from her dripping brow. As each batter came up to the plate, her teammates rallied behind her, and Bella poured her heart and soul into her pitch. Digging deep in her spirit to give her best focus, she helped her team bring the score to a tie.

Bella and her teammates gave it all they had. But, in the end, the other team scored the run that broke the championship game tie, and Bella's team lost the game. In defeat, Bella and her teammates walked off the softball field.

As they approached the dugout, upset from the heat and the loss, their families and friends greeted them with smiling faces, shouts, and applause. Suddenly, they saw the supportive fans rise in a standing ovation. Bella and her teammates realized how much their effort and sportswomanship had touched the hearts of so many. And, in this realization, they felt victorious.

Revilo ran to Bella and jumped up and licked her cheek. Bella's parents, friends, and family members hugged her and told her how proud they were of her unwavering determination and the love and respect she had for her supportive coaches and teammates. They were even more proud of her for the love she had for herself.

Bella did not let the loss of the game break her spirit. She knew that her worth was not defined by a single championship game. That knowing came from within. In addition to her speech impediment, being taller than the other kids her age had always made Bella stand out, sometimes in ways that made her feel picked on, and other times in ways that made her feel special. Being tall, while at the same time humble and compassionate, attracted others to her for guidance. Little by little, without realizing it, Bella was stepping into her God-given ability as a leader.

She continued to accept the parts of her that were different and began to understand that her differences were the things that made her unique and special.

Bella began working with a speech therapist to strengthen her ability to pronounce the letters that challenged her. She used her voice to speak up for others who faced similar speech challenges.

Her path had not been an easy one. There were times when she felt like giving up and quitting, and times when she cried. But she persevered through the challenges, because she believed in herself. And, in the process, she grew stronger.

The Korean language has a word for the perseverance that Bella had. It is "Enye".

The following year, Bella tried out to pitch in the Gold level championship games with the Vipers team, and she made it. In fact, she was picked two years in a row. Her vision of herself on the pitcher's mound of a professional softball stadium, surrounded by cheering fans, watching her throw the perfect underhand fast pitch had come true.

In doing what she loved, in following her knowing, and in her commitment to practicing and playing, Bella learned many invaluable lessons. She learned about sportsmanship— or sportswomanship,— compassionate leadership, confidence, perseverance, and much more. The most important lesson Bella learned was to accept, support, and love her teammates. She learned that it was about playing together and remembering to have fun. And whenever she picked up a paintbrush or stepped onto a softball field, she carried with her the lessons she had learned.

Years later, after playing hundreds of games of softball, Bella returned to her other love and became a renowned landscape artist, sharing her beautiful paintings with people around the world. She had turned both passions into reality.

Bella's journey taught her the true meaning of perseverance, confidence, trust, and unconditional love for oneself. In following her passions, Bella spread love and acceptance wherever she went and continued to inspire others with her story of inner resilience and self-belief.

To the Inner Child in You

Life is not about winning or losing. It is about choosing to follow what lights you up and having faith and determination to do what matters. It's about what happens when you walk your journey in confidence, acceptance, and unconditional love.

Bella's story serves as a reminder to all of us to never to be ashamed of who we are and always love and accept all our pieces and parts. Our differences are what make us special. With determination and love, we can achieve anything we set our minds to.

So, dear ones, when you face challenges or begin to doubt yourself, remember Bella. Embrace your uniqueness, believe in your dreams, and never let anyone make you feel small. With trust, confidence, acceptance, and unconditional love of yourself and others, you can create your own inspiring story, just like Bella did.

About the Author

Meet Patricia Garza Pinto,

a Holistic Health and Wellness
Practitioner empowering individuals,
particularly "SiSTARS,"
to confront and transform
their emotional and physical pain.
Drawing from personal struggles,
Patricia guides others on their journey
of healing and self-discovery.
Patricia lives in Idyllwild, California.

For more information on Patricia's services,
including private and holistic healing retreats,

Visit
www.divineyourpower.co

Milton Keynes UK
Ingram Content Group UK Ltd.
UKHW050638241124
451508UK00009B/76

Diabetes

© Aladdin Books 1989

Designed and produced by
Aladdin Books Ltd
70 Old Compton Street
London W1V 5PA

First published in
Great Britain in 1989 by
Franklin Watts Ltd
96 Leonard Street
London EC2A 4RH

Design: David West Children's Book Design
Editor: Zuza Vrbova
Picture Research: Cecilia Weston-Baker
Illustrator: Stuart Brendon

Consultant: Dr Alan Davies MD., MRCP Research Fellow in Child Health, University of Bristol, UK; Medical Affairs Manager, Novo Laboratories Ltd., UK.

ISBN 0-7496-0044-6

Printed in Belgium

CONTENTS

WHAT IS DIABETES	4
DIABETIC DISORDERS	8
TREATMENT OF DIABETES	12
LIVING WITH DIABETES	20
TAKING CARE OF YOUR BODY	28
GLOSSARY	31
INDEX	32

Diabetes

Barbara Taylor

FRANKLIN WATTS
London : New York : Toronto : Sydney

WHAT IS DIABETES?

People with diabetes have too much glucose in their blood. The full name of the disorder is diabetes mellitus, which means "a passing of honeysweet urine". The term "diabetes", from 18th century Latin, comes from the fact that untreated diabetes makes the body pass urine that contains sugar.

Glucose comes from food we eat. Foods that contain sugar, called carbohydrates, are broken down into more simple sugars such as a substitute called glucose. Glucose is the body's main fuel. It is "burned" to produce energy, to keep the body working.

Two main chemical messengers, called hormones, act to keep the amount of glucose in the blood at a constant level. These hormones are insulin and glucagon. Insulin decreases the amount of glucose in the blood and glucagon increases it. Insulin and glucagon both play a vital role. If a person has too little insulin, the amount of glucose builds up in the blood and diabetes will develop.

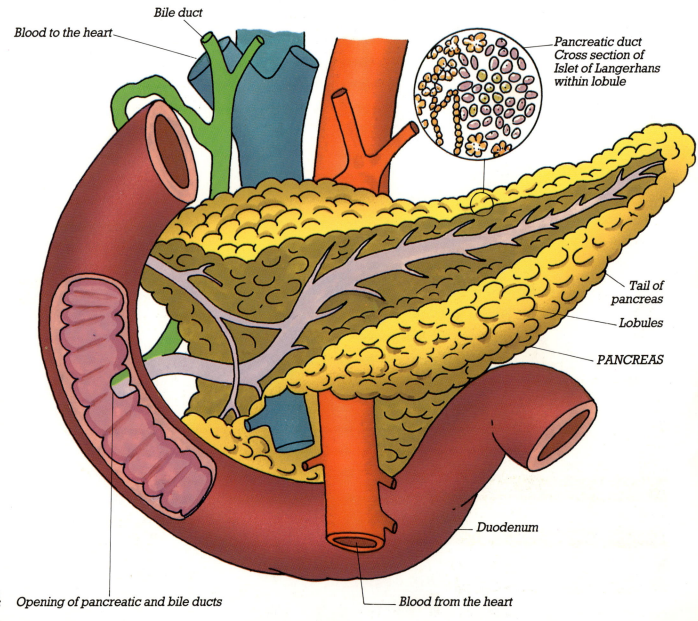

Islets of Langerhans

Insulin and glucagon are made in special groups of cells scattered throughout the pancreas, a pear shaped gland located below the liver. These cells look like small islands and were called islets by Langerhans, the scientist who discovered them. The word *insulin* comes from the Latin word for islet.

There are three kinds of cells in the islets – alpha cells, beta cells and delta cells. Alpha cells make glucagon, the hormone which releases glucose from the liver. This raises the amount of glucose in the blood when the body needs energy. The beta cells, on the other hand, make insulin, which opens pathways into cells so that glucose can enter cells to be used or stored. Insulin works in the opposite way to glucagon and decreases the amount of glucose in the blood. Delta cells produce a hormone called somatostatin which suppresses insulin and glucagon.

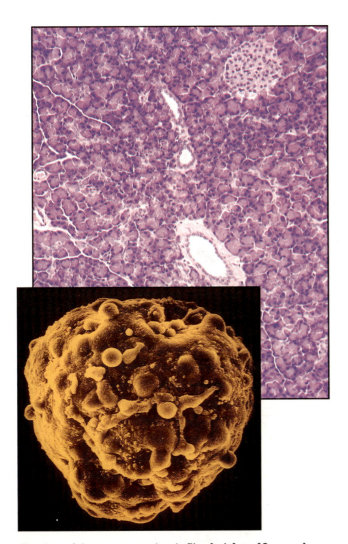

Section of the pancreas (top). Single islet of Langerhans.

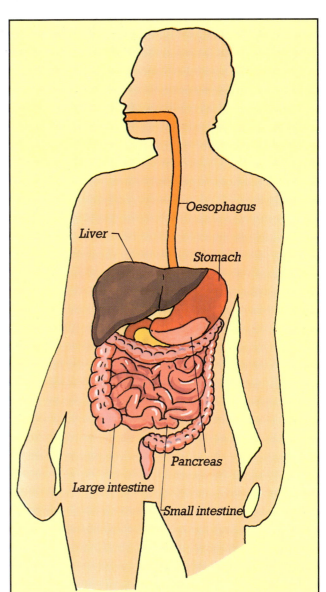

The pancreas

The pancreas is a large gland in the abdomen just behind the stomach. It has two main jobs. In the islets of Langerhans, it makes insulin and glucagon. Both hormones are released straight into the bloodstream and circulate. There are about one million islets in the pancreas. Insulin is released from the beta cells in the pancreas, after a meal, as a direct response to the rise in the level of glucose in the blood.

Other cells in the pancreas make digestive juices. These contain enzymes that help to digest food. Every day, the pancreas pours out between ½ – 1 litre (1-2 pints) of digestive juices down a tube which leads into the small intestine to break down the food.

Normal production of Insulin

After a meal, glucose from the breakdown of food (digestion) is absorbed through the wall of the intestine into the bloodstream. The resulting high levels of glucose in the blood make the islet cells in the pancreas produce more insulin. Insulin travels in the blood with glucose and helps glucose go into muscle cells, which need energy from glucose to work. Any extra glucose is converted into glycogen and stored in the liver and muscles. Insulin is essential for this process, and afterwards, the glucose level in the blood reduces to normal. As a result, the islet cells stop producing so much insulin – until the next meal.

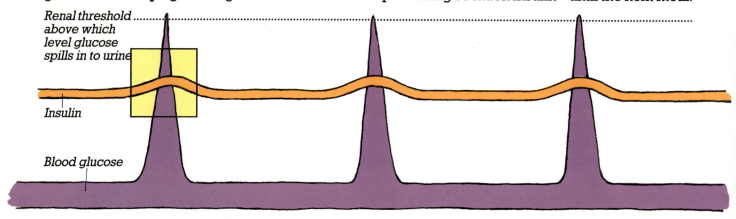

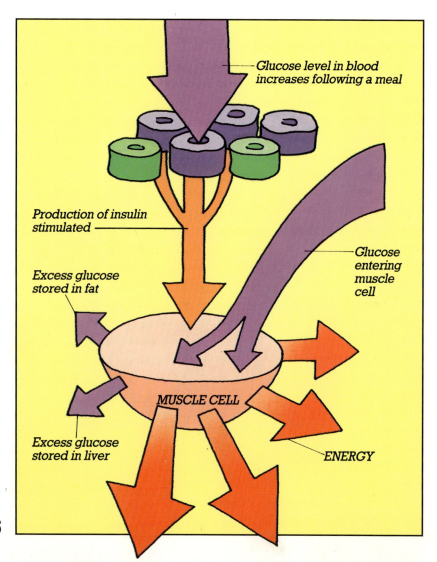

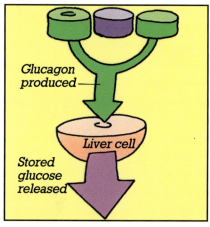

Insulin is produced whenever the glucose level in the blood is too high. Insulin cuts down the glucose level by helping some cells to store energy and other cells to burn glucose to release energy. Glucagon is produced if there is too little glucose in the blood. Glucagon increases blood glucose by making the liver turn some of its glycogen stores into glucose. Over a longer period of time, glucagon may turn proteins into glucose.

The diabetic cycle

In a person with diabetes, insufficient glucose is produced or the insulin does not function normally in the body. The body's cells cannot use or store glucose efficiently. As a result, the blood glucose level goes up and up. This condition is called *hyperglycaemia*, and means "excess blood glucose".

The excess glucose is passed out in the urine, and the liver releases glucose stores; some of this glucose is also lost in the urine. The cells start to burn up fats and proteins to obtain energy and the person loses weight.

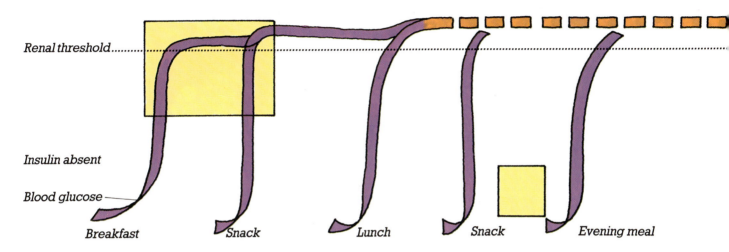

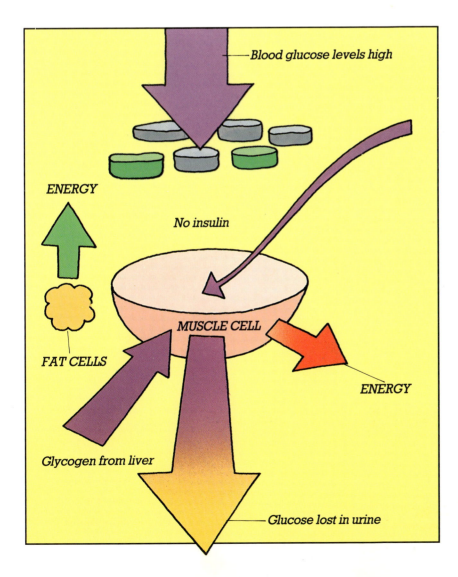

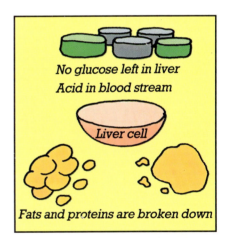

In diabetes, the body's cells cannot use glucose properly. The liver therefore releases stores of glucose into the blood. With every meal, the level of glucose goes up and up. The lack of insulin means that fat has to be broken down to provide energy. Substances called ketones, which smell like nail polish remover, are also produced. The blood becomes acidic and the person may develop diabetic keto-acidosis or "ketosis".

DIABETIC DISORDERS

Nobody knows the real cause of diabetes. About 1 child in 700, or one child in an average secondary school has diabetes. Diabetes is common and different types occur at any age. About 1 or 2 in every 100 people have some type of diabetes.

Diabetes cannot be "caught", like people catch mumps or chickenpox. Insulin-dependent diabetes, the most dramatic kind and the most common in young people, develops because the beta cells in the pancreas are slowly damaged. The cells cannot grow again. People with diabetes have it for the rest of their lives.

Most diabetes is an inherited disorder, in that a tendency to develop diabetes is inherited. Sometimes, but not always, the symptoms of diabetes are brought out by an infection of severe stress. The discovery and isolation of insulin in 1922 has enabled many thousands of people with diabetes to live and lead normal and fulfilled lives.

Symptoms

One of the earliest clues to diabetes is the frequent passing of large amounts of urine. This makes the person feel thirsty because of the liquids lost in their urine. Other symptoms include weight loss, tiredness, blurred vision, vomiting and tingling in the hands and feet. There are two main types of diabetes. In insulin-dependent diabetes, which occurs in younger people, the person makes little or no insulin. In non-insulin-dependent diabetes, which occurs in older people, the person does not produce enough insulin to deal with the glucose in the blood.

In insulin-dependent diabetes, the symptoms usually develop over a few weeks. The symptoms of non-insulin-dependent diabetes take longer to develop, and some adults do not notice any symptoms.

If there is a severe lack of insulin, or somebody who is taking insulin stops taking it, symptoms will return. Rarely, symptoms of diabetic keto-acidosis will develop. This is because fat is broken down into ketones, which are poisonous in large amounts. Hospital treatment is needed. Lack of insulin can also occur if the person has an infection or injury, such as a broken bone, because the body needs more insulin to fight the illness.

Symptoms include thirst, weight loss and blurred vision.

Insulin-dependent diabetes

Originally called "juvenile onset diabetes", this is now called insulin-dependent diabetes, Type I diabetes, or IDDM (insulin-dependent diabetes mellitus). Little or no insulin is made in the pancreas. Therefore insulin has to be given by injection every day. This form of diabetes usually starts to affect people when they are under 40 years of age. It affects about 3 to 4 people in every 1,000 people aged between 20 and 40 years. Men and women are equally likely to suffer from this type of diabetes. Sometimes an illness, such as chickenpox or a broken bone, will make the disease appear. But, the disease is not caused by any illness.

The type of food a person eats or anything else a person likes to do is not related to the cause of insulin-dependent diabetes. The first appearance of this type of diabetes can be dramatic, including passing of large amounts of urine, excessive thirst, weight loss and tiredness. The symptoms can develop quickly, although they are usually fairly obvious, and not difficult to diagnose. However, when looking back, families are often surprised at how long the person with diabetes has had the symptoms. A small number of cases have no hereditary component. Environmental factors – pregnancy, weight stress, diet – may trigger or bring on the symptoms of the disease.

Non-insulin-dependent diabetes

Originally called "maturity onset diabetes", this is now called non-insulin-dependent diabetes, Type II diabetes, or NIDDM (non-insulin-dependent diabetes mellitus). About three quarters of all people with diabetes have this sort. The pancreas makes some insulin but not enough to deal with all the glucose in the blood. This form can usually be treated with tablets and a controlled diet. The tablets encourage more insulin to be produced. Some people who develop this type are overweight and most know someone in their family with diabetes. The symptoms tend to develop more slowly, and are not as severe as those for insulin-dependent diabetes.

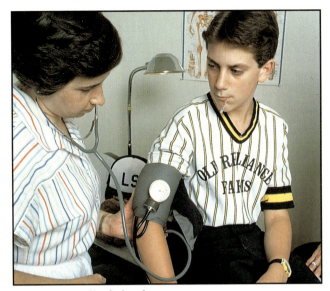
A routine medical check

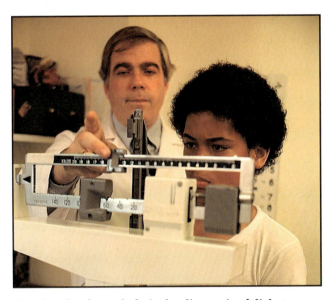
Regular check-ups help in the diagnosis of diabetes.

Older, overweight people may develop diabetes.

Hypoglycaemia

A low level of blood glucose is called "hypoglycaemia", often shortened to "hypo". *Hypo*, from the Greek, means under and *glycaemia* means blood glucose. "Hypos" can happen if a meal is delayed or exercise is unexpected, unusual or prolonged. "Hypos" can occur also without any obvious cause. When blood glucose levels fall, the body puts its own rescue system into action and releases emergency hormones, for example adrenaline. When the blood glucose level is very low, the brain does not receive enough glucose to work properly. This can lead to a feeling of strangeness and sometimes difficulty in concentrating. Very rarely, and only if the blood glucose level is extremely low, a "hypo" can lead to convulsions.

The emergency hormones raise the level of glucose. Adrenaline also makes a person sweat and the heart beat more rapidly. Glucagon can be given to bring a person out of a bad "hypo".

"Hypos" usually occur quickly, in a matter of minutes. A person with diabetes often recognizes the signs of a "hypo" before it is obvious to anyone else. The "hypo" can then quickly be stopped by eating or drinking something sweet. All those with diabetes should carry some form of sugar for emergencies.

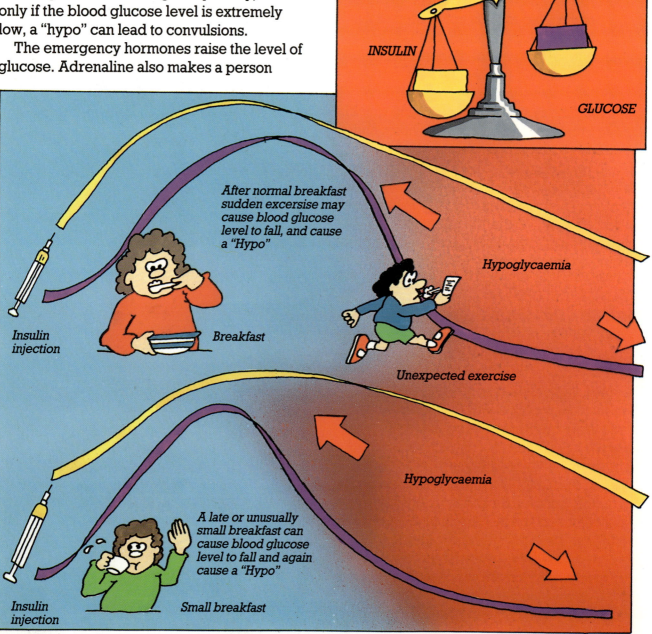

Possible complications

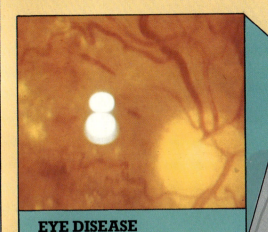
EYE DISEASE

Diabetes can affect the eyes, the kidneys, the heart and the nerves. It may affect eyes because blood vessels in the retina can be damaged. An expert can spot these changes early and treat them to prevent problems with eyesight.

Blood vessels in the kidney can be damaged. Urine tests will detect this problem. Sometimes people have to take tablets for kidney problems.

HEART DISEASE

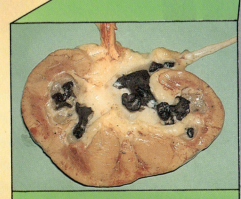
KIDNEY DISEASE

The arteries can become "furred up" with fatty deposits which slow the flow of blood to the heart. This is the reason people with diabetes should pay particular attention to having plenty of exercise and healthy eating.

Long-term diabetes may damage the nerves and cause feelings of numbness in the feet. If this happens, a person with diabetes may injure or burn their feet. This problem is connected to diabetes affecting the nervous system.

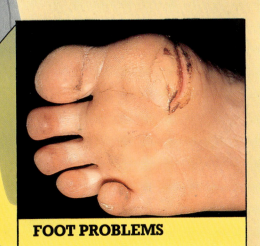
FOOT PROBLEMS

TREATMENT OF DIABETES

There is no cure for diabetes. But it can be treated so that a diabetic can lead a normal life and do most of the things that anybody else can. Treatment has to be kept up every day throughout life to avoid the symptoms that go with high or low blood glucose levels, and the possible risk of comas. Treatment cuts down the risk of health problems later in life. Complications in pregnancy are also less likely if diabetes is controlled.

There are three main ways of treating diabetes: by changes in diet alone, by diet and tablets, and by diet and injections of insulin. Regular exercise is an important part of any treatment because it lowers the amount of glucose in the blood. Regular checks on the levels of glucose in the blood and urine are essential to make sure the treatment is keeping the levels normal. Treatment of diabetes has become so successful that most people lead a full and normal life.

Diagnosis of diabetes

If a person has any of the symptoms of diabetes, such as excessive thirst, passing large amounts of urine or losing weight, a doctor may suspect that diabetes is the cause. A simple blood or urine test for glucose will make sure. An abnormally high level of glucose points to diabetes. Normally, there is no glucose in the urine. So if a person's urine does contain glucose, it usually means that the person has diabetes. Sometimes the diagnosis may come as a complete surprise because there may be no other symptoms of the disorder, or only mild ones. A child with diabetes may look tired, thin and listless and may well complain of being excessively thirsty. The excess sugar results in frequent passing of urine. This may cause bed-wetting in some children, and incontinence in elderly people.

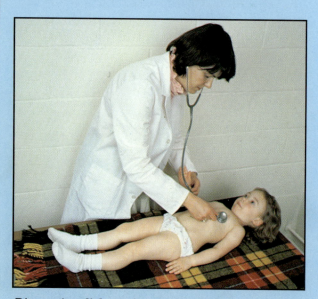
Diagnosing diabetes in a young girl

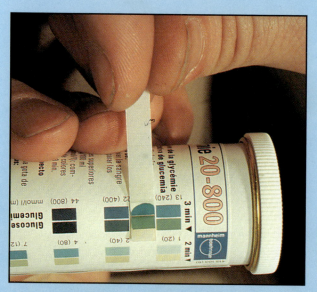
Diabetes test strip for counting glucose levels

Insulin-dependent diabetes

Before the early 1920s and the discovery of the insulin hormone, the diagnosis of diabetes meant a very strict diet and a difficult lifestyle. The first person to describe the effect of injecting insulin was the Rumanian doctor, Nicola Paolescu. This discovery was followed up by the Canadians, Banting and Best, who in collaboration with Macleod and Collip developed the use of injecting insulin for human patients.

Since then, insulin treatment has saved millions of lives. Insulin injections replace the insulin which the person with diabetes is unable to produce. Unfortunately, insulin is a protein. It cannot be swallowed as tablets because it would be destroyed by digestive juices. It has to be injected straight into the body, usually just under the skin. If injections are repeatedly given at the same spot the fatty tissue changes and the insulin is not absorbed properly. For this reason, it is important to change the injection site at every injection.

There are two main types of insulin: fast-acting and slow-acting. Fast-acting insulin is clear and is called soluble or regular insulin. Its maximum effect is about 2 hours after the injection and its effect fades after about 4 hours. Slow-acting insulin, which is cloudy, works over a longer time period. The effects usually last for 12-14 hours, although some types last for 24 hours. Long acting insulin provides a background level of insulin between meals.

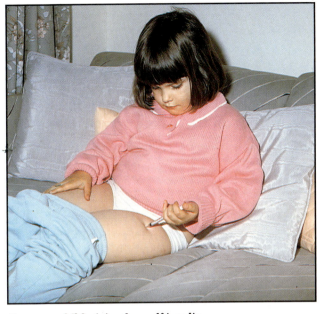

A young child giving herself insulin

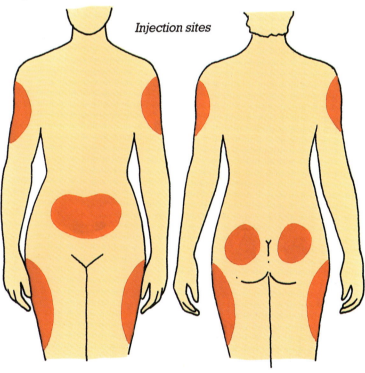

Injection sites

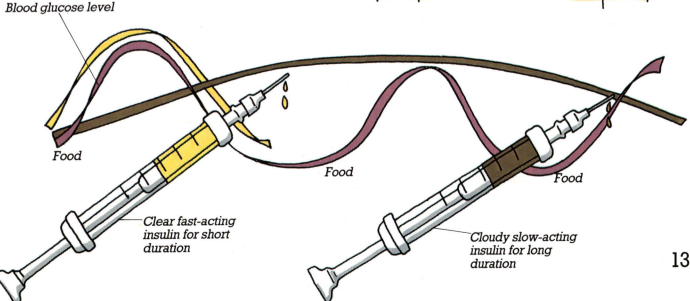

Blood glucose level

Food

Clear fast-acting insulin for short duration

Food

Food

Cloudy slow-acting insulin for long duration

Maintaining glucose levels

Regular checks on glucose levels in the blood and urine are important. A drop of blood can be obtained with a sterile needle or an automatic pricking device. The blood is placed on a special paper test strip, which changes colour. To estimate the glucose level, the colour is compared with a colour scale or put inside a special meter. Urine tests involve adding a tablet to a sample of urine, or placing a strip of paper in the urine to see the colour change. The results of these tests, as well as insulin doses, body weight and any "hypos" need to be recorded for the people at the clinic to discuss with you. Isolated tests of urine are of little value in ascertaining whether a person's diabetes is well controlled. But, a regular record of tests gives a much better idea of the real level of control.

Pricking finger

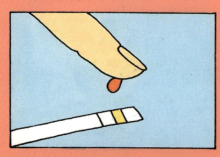

Putting blood sample onto a test strip

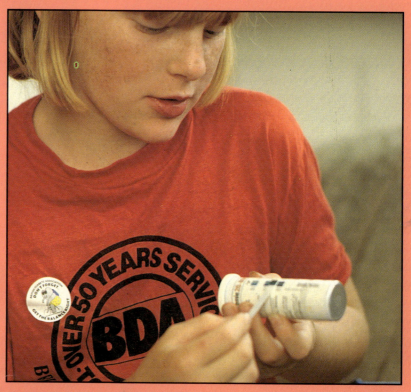

Testing urine according to colour changes

It is a good idea to keep regular records of levels of blood and urine.

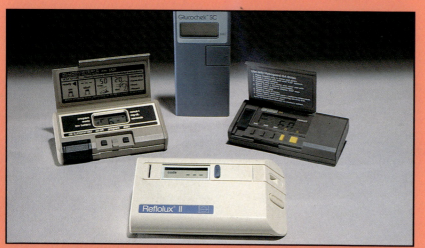

Modern meters provide accurate glucose level readings

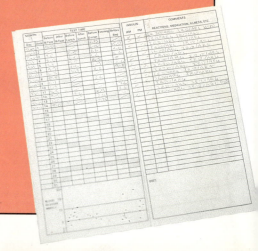

Food and diet

For all types of diabetes, diet is one of the most important methods of controlling the disorder. A "diabetic diet" is not a special diet, more a healthy, balanced mixture of carbohydrates, fats and proteins – which is good for anybody.

High-fibre carbohydrates should be an important part of the diet, and fatty and salty foods should be avoided. Sweet, sugary foods should be reduced except during illness or emergencies such as a "hypo".

"Diabetic" foods are usually sweet because the sugar has been replaced by artificial sweeteners. It is best to avoid these foods because the sweeteners may cause tummy pain and diarrhoea if eaten in large amounts.

Exercise

Exercise burns up energy and lowers the level of glucose in the blood. So it cuts down the amount of insulin needed. Exercise also makes insulin work more efficiently which makes controlling the amount of glucose in the blood easier. However, it is important to take care to adjust eating habits and insulin according to the changes that take place in the body as a result of exercise. When it is necessary to do a lot of energetic work or take a lot of exercise, reduce the insulin dose or eat more carbohydrate.

Go ahead

Stop

Treatment for non-insulin-dependent diabetes

This type of diabetes may be controlled with a weight reducing diet which will lower the level of glucose in the blood. This also makes the insulin in the body work more efficiently. Some people also need to take tablets to stimulate the manufacture of more insulin, but these people must try to keep their weight down. Occasionally, insulin is also needed. The aim in the treatment of non-insulin-dependent diabetes is to reach a point where the naturally-produced insulin maintains the blood sugar at a normal level.

Treatment of hypoglycaemia

If the glucose level in the blood becomes so low that an attack of hypoglycaemia occurs (a "hypo"), the affected person should stop what they are doing. This is especially important if they are doing something that might put themselves or others at risk, such as driving a car or using machinery or climbing a ladder. The person should eat or drink something sweet. Sugar lumps, glucose tablets, biscuits or glucose drinks are all useful because the glucose they contain can be quickly absorbed into the blood. Within a few minutes, the symptoms should disappear. If they do not, the treatment should be repeated after 10 minutes. Another treatment is a sugar gel, squeezed around the gums.

If the diabetic becomes unconscious, treatment is usually more difficult. It is important not to try to push sweet things down the person's throat, because the food may cause choking. Give the hormone glucagon by injection. It is very easy to use, and all family and close friends of people with diabetes should know how to use it.

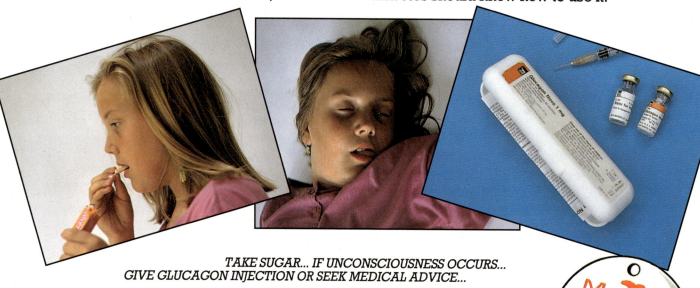

TAKE SUGAR... IF UNCONSCIOUSNESS OCCURS... GIVE GLUCAGON INJECTION OR SEEK MEDICAL ADVICE...

Information for others

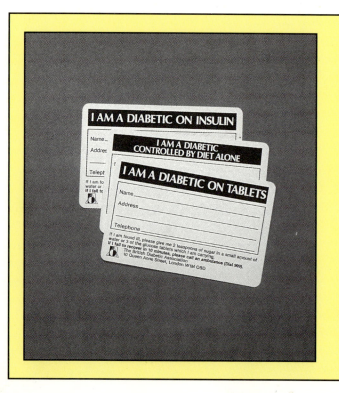

All people with diabetes should carry some form of identification with their name, address and telephone number, as well as instructions for treating a "hypo". A special Medic-Alert bracelet or pendant (as above) contains the phone number of an office where records of the person are kept. An SOS talisman can be worn as a pendant or on a watch strap. It contains a strip of paper with medical details. If a person has a "hypo", call for a doctor or an ambulance. Many ambulance drivers are trained to give injections of glucagon.

Pen therapy

Many insulin-dependent patients with diabetes are now injecting insulin using a new kind of device which looks like a pen. Like an ink pen, it contains a cartridge of insulin but the cartridge is filled with insulin rather than ink. The most common kind contains cartridges of soluble, fast-acting, insulin. The pen is used every day to provide the exact dose of insulin required. Long-acting insulin is injected using a conventional syringe to cover a person's night-time insulin requirements and the meal time requirements during the day are covered by injections using the pen. This method mimics the normal non-diabetic secretion of insulin by the pancreas. As insulin is produced naturally in response to eating, the golden rule is: if you *don't* eat, you *don't* inject; if you *do eat* you *do inject*. Other similar kinds of pen devices will be available shortly that will contain long-acting and pre-mixed insulins for different and varying insulin needs. Using pen therapy gives people with diabetes many advantages. They are able to lead a more flexible lifestyle. Using a pen makes the injection of insulin much easier than using a syringe.

A "pen" for giving insulin

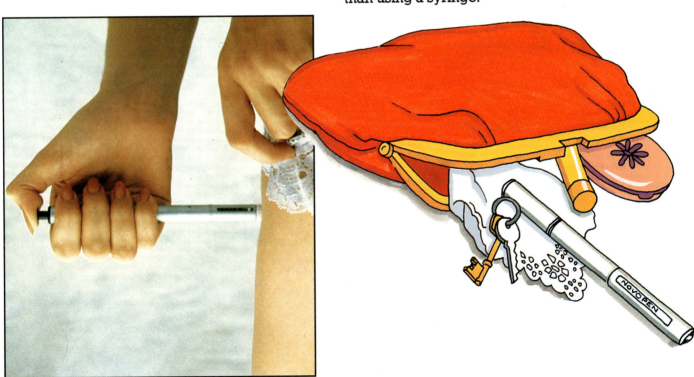

There are many advantages to the new pen type of injection. It is easier to use and to carry round.

With care and experience the use of a pen can give better control of the level of glucose in the blood.

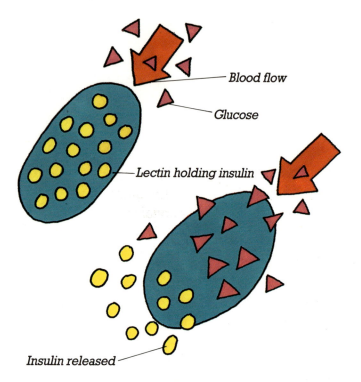

- Blood flow
- Glucose
- Lectin holding insulin
- Insulin released

Other alternatives to injections

For many years, scientists have been trying to prepare a type of insulin that does not have to be injected. Some researchers have tried coating the insulin in fatty globules made of chemicals such as lectin. These stop the insulin from being digested by juices in the stomach. The fatty coating eventually dissolves, so that insulin is released into the bloodstream.

Other researchers are working on ways of blowing insulin up the nose with a special spray. The problem with giving insulin by mouth or nose is that it is hard to know exactly how much of the dose has been absorbed into the bloodstream. As yet, inhalants have not been found to be accurate enough to control the balancing act between high and low blood glucose levels that is needed with diabetes.

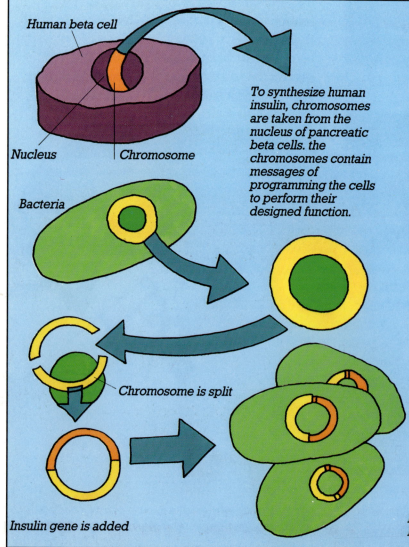

- Human beta cell
- Nucleus
- Chromosome
- Bacteria
- Chromosome is split
- Insulin gene is added

To synthesize human insulin, chromosomes are taken from the nucleus of pancreatic beta cells. the chromosomes contain messages of programming the cells to perform their designed function.

Making human insulin

Human insulin can now be made in the laboratory by means of genetic engineering. The technique uses a bacterium called *Escherichia coli* or bakers yeast, which has been specially bred for use in the laboratory. Whichever organism is used, the genetic code for insulin is inserted into the nucleus of the host cell. The organism then makes insulin while going about its normal daily tasks!

The insulin is isolated from the fermentation broth of the organism. This is done in a similar way to that of alcohol being purified from home-made beer. The insulin is identical to human insulin in every way but does not come anywhere near a human until it is injected. There is, therefore, no risk of catching any disease, such as hepatitis or AIDS, from human insulin.

Insulin gene in chromosome is replaced in bacterium and grown in culture medium

Artificial pancreas

Scientists hope that one day it may be possible to implant an artificial pancreas into diabetics. It would be placed into the abdominal cavity rather than under the skin of the abdomen or chest, and refilled with insulin either daily or weekly.

An artifical pancreas is a machine that pumps insulin into the blood. It has a tiny sensor to measure the amount of gluocose in the body tissues. This information is fed to a microcomputer, which tells an insulin pump to release insulin into the blood whenever it is needed. The device mimics the workings of a natural pancreas, although the real gland is much more complex and is able to control insulin levels in the body in a more subtle way.

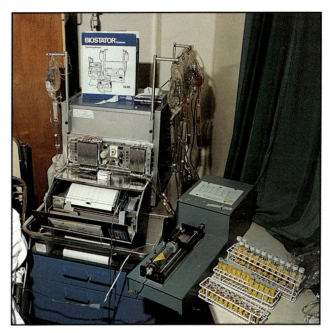

A blood analysis machine

Pancreatic transplants

Attempts to transplant part of a normal pancreas into someone with diabetes have not been very successful. The operation is a difficult one and only about 40 per cent of the transplanted organs are still working. One major problem is that some way has to be found to stop the digestive juices leaking out and digesting the insulin.

Pancreatic transplants have mainly been attempted in patients who have kidney failure due to the diabetes. Since the pancreas lies up against one of the kidneys, it is technically possible to transplant the two organs together, simultaneously. But, this operation has only ever been attempted a few times.

A possibly more promising hope for the future is transplanting just the islet cells. They could be injected into the abdomen without any surgery. The problem is how to stop the body from recognizing them as foreign cells and trying to destroy them. Tiny jelly-like beads have been developed to protect the islet cells from white blood cells, which would otherwise attack the islet cells and gobble them up. But, the insulin can still seep out through the beads.

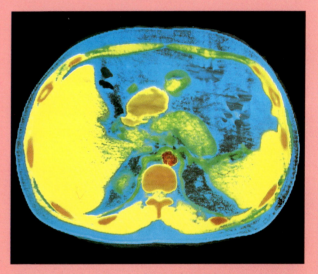

X-ray scan showing the liver, pancreas and spleen

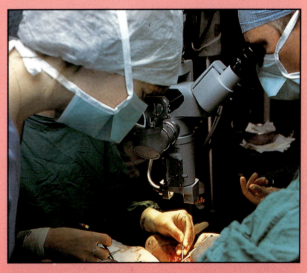

Two surgeons transplanting islet cells

LIVING WITH DIABETES

Nobody likes having diabetes. When people are first told they have diabetes, they usually feel shocked, frightened, depressed or angry that it has happened to them. Parents may feel guilty and blame themselves. This is a natural emotional reaction. Understanding what we know about the cause of diabetes can help some people. Some people find it hard to cope with the feeling of being different from others, but most soon become adjusted and carry on with their own lives. Diabetes does not prevent most people from doing most things. Eventually, most people learn to live with diabetes and do not allow it to stop them enjoying life. If a diabetic leads a healthy lifestyle – eating the correct foods and taking plenty of exercise – and keeps blood glucose levels under control, there is no reason why they should not lead a full, exciting and active life. This includes an interesting job or career, playing sports and going on holidays – just like anyone else.

Adjusting to a diagnosis of diabetes

Most people take a while to come to terms with having diabetes. There is a lot to learn, and it is easy to panic and feel helpless. It is all too easy to blame diabetes for the problems of daily life which have nothing to do with diabetes. If a person is found to have diabetes, it is best to take things slowly at first and ask questions. There is always help available, and the more people know about their own diabetes, the better they can look after themselves. Some people's personality may become more pronounced during adjustment to the disorder. Older people may find diabetes a shock and a great upset to their usual lifestyle.

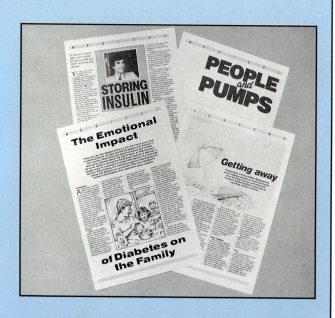

Talking to clinic staff and other people can often be helpful. It is reassuring to discover that other people share the same worries and have overcome similar problems. The clinic team are experienced and you can always seek further advice from social workers if there are problems at home. It helps people if they understand the causes of diabetes and to know some basic facts about food and how it is digested normally.

Having injections

Everybody is bothered by the thought of giving themselves injections for the rest of their lives. However, most people soon learn to accept this part of having diabetes.

It can be difficult to explain to children why injections are necessary. All parents have to find their own way of doing this; it is important to be honest. When children have learned to inject themselves they can then become more independent. For example, they can stay with Granny, and this can be a useful stimulus. Many first learn to inject on holiday camps with other children.

Many children give their own injections, although their parents may want to check the dose for them. Most children find it is less painful to give their own injections. It is important not to push anyone to give injections if they really don't want to. Many very young children do give their injections themselves.

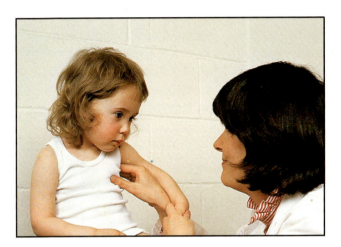

Teaching a child about diabetes

Practising injecting fruit or a doll helps a child to learn the technique of giving injections

FEAR OF PROBLEMS IN THE NIGHT

Everybody is scared of having a "hypo" while asleep. Usually, the early symptoms will wake a person with diabetes up. They will wake up feeling hungry and sweating. Sometimes it is possible to sleep through a "hypo". The person may wake with a headache and may find nightclothes soaked in sweat. The body recognizes the problem automatically and increases the release of glucose from the liver. At the same time the body releases other emergency hormones such as adrenaline. This hormone helps to raise the blood glucose but has other effects too – it makes you sweat and makes your heart beat faster. It is important to tell the clinic about night "hypos" so that a problem can be dealt with and overcome.

Problems in the home

Problems will always occur at home because the person with diabetes has to do different things from the rest of the family. Parents sometimes say that it is a bit like having a new baby in the house again because they worry more, especially at night. All children need to feel that their parents understand the problems of having diabetes but they also need to know that they can cope well on their own. Children with diabetes are no different from all other children in wanting both understanding and independence at the same time. Certainly, feeling sorry for someone rarely helps. It is best if parents – and brothers and sisters – can make a child with diabetes feel like any other child.

Sometimes people use illness as an excuse for bad or irritable behaviour, or to avoid facing up to things. Young adults may rebel against all the things they have to do to manage their diabetes. This is because diabetes makes them different from their friends. Most parents realize that laying down rigid rules does not help, and that it is often best to ignore occasional outbursts and tantrums, and try to understand the problems of diabetes.

Illness

After an illness, injury or a surgical operation, the stress hormones the body produces to fight the illness make the blood glucose level increase. This happens even if the person does not eat or vomits and finds it hard to keep food down. During a stay in hospital, patients become worried, have a different diet and may be unable to exercise. All of these things raise the level of glucose in the blood. More insulin than normal is needed to cope with the extra glucose. The clinic will advise how much extra insulin is needed.

If someone is too ill to eat, he or she should drink fluids such as milk or fruit juice, and take plenty of sugar-free liquids too. Whatever, a diabetic who normally takes insulin should never stop taking insulin. If insulin is stopped, the body will start breaking down fats to release glucose and the person with diabetes may become even more ill.

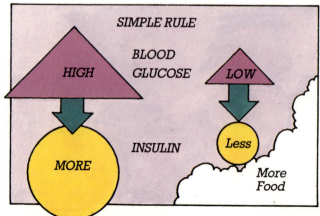

School

If a pupil is diagnosed as having diabetes, it is important to tell the head teacher, form teacher and school nurse. The clinic nurse will usually visit the school to discuss all aspects of diabetes with the relevant teachers. If the child has a "hypo", the teachers should be aware of the symptoms and know what to do. Occasionally teachers, particularly the games teacher, will carry glucose so they can help quickly if there is a problem. Most children with diabetes will need to eat something before taking vigorous exercise. On school trips, a pupil with diabetes should take plenty of spare food and drink, as well as a testing kit and insulin. This will avoid problems if the trip is delayed. At school, a child should be encouraged to take part in all school activities. Most schools will have at least one pupil with diabetes. School information packs such as those produced by Diabetic Associations (shown below) are useful to help staff understand diabetes. Most of the problems in schools arise from lack of communication. For example a new member of staff being unaware of, and having no experience with diabetes.

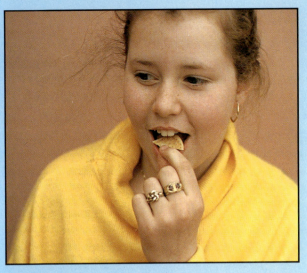

A diabetic may sometimes need to eat a snack in class to maintain blood glucose level.

School meals usually provide a well-balanced diet

A child with diabetes can participate in school sports along with other children.

23

Work

People with diabetes can take up most jobs and careers, as long as the diabetes is well controlled. It is best to be open and honest about the disease on job application forms and in interviews. It is also very important that colleagues know about the diabetes. They should know what to do if a "hypo" happens.

A few jobs are not open to insulin-dependent diabetics. For example, they are not allowed to fly aircraft or drive a bus or a heavy goods vehicle. The armed services, police force and fire service do not accept insulin-dependent diabetics. If somebody develops diabetes after joining the armed services, he or she is usually kept on but may be transferred to a different job. These restrictions are to make sure that if a person with diabetes has a "hypo" he or she is not injured while at work or put other people at risk. Dangerous jobs, such as deep-sea diving or steel erecting, are possible for confident, well controlled people who can keep their diabetes under control as well. For people with non-insulin-dependent diabetes, the condition has no effect on their work whatsoever. Even shift work should not pose any problems.

Driving

Most people with diabetes are able to drive a car. The main problem is the possibility of having a "hypo" while driving. If a "hypo" comes on while driving, slow down, stop safely and eat something sweet straight away. It is important not to resume the journey until the driver feels completely normal again. A person with diabetes should keep a supply of biscuits or glucose in the car.

Holidays

There is more chance of "hypos" happening on holiday because of the change of routine – unfamiliar exercise, delayed meals or exposure to cold and wet. Some people carry an identity card, necklace or bracelet (see page 16). It is wise to take tablets to prevent travel sickness because vomiting after injecting insulin may cause "hypos".

Take all the insulin needed for the holiday period. In different countries, insulins are often of a different type, strength or purity. All the insulin manufacturers will tell you what is available in every country. In some remote places it may be impossible to obtain insulin at all. The British Embassy, High Commission or local American Express office are usually very helpful if your last insulin supply has dropped into the Orinoco. Always carry glucose and make sure you are not separated from your insulin. Carry insulin in the cabin hold of the aeroplane as it may freeze in the luggage compartment. Insulin is stable for a period of two or three weeks, and does not need to be kept in the fridge during a holiday.

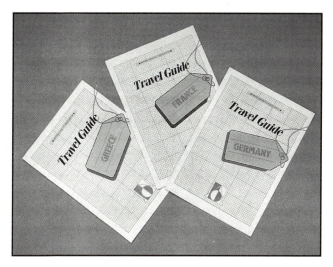

Guidelines on travelling in various countries are available for those with diabetes

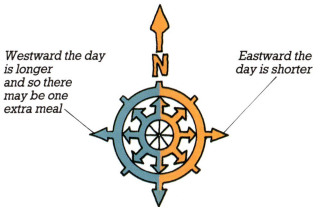

Time zone changes may affect people with diabetes in terms of insulin requirements and food, when travelling

Time zone changes cause problems on long flights. Going eastwards makes the day shorter and going westwards makes the day longer. The time affects the number of meals and the timing of injections. For example, travelling by air from the United Kingdom to the United States, extra insulin and food will be needed on the journey.

Some people avoid the problem by leaving their watches set to the time of the country they are travelling from. They can then eat their own packed meals and give insulin at the usual times. Coping with time zone changes depends on the type and dose of insulin, and it is best to ask the clinic for advice. Do not be put off travelling because of diabetes. Remember, there are diabetics all over the world.

Regular check-ups

It is important for a person with diabetes to visit a diabetic clinic at regular intervals. This applies even if a person has their diabetes well controlled and has no problems. A good clinic will be a partner in your journey with diabetes. Professional people can help you when times are bad, and share in your joy when times are good. There are all sorts of people with special skills at clinics, including specialist diabetes nurses, dietitians, chiropodists, eye specialists, social workers and doctors. The people at the clinic have their own specialized skills.

Diabetes needs a lot of self-discipline, and regular visits to a clinic can help to develop regular discipline.

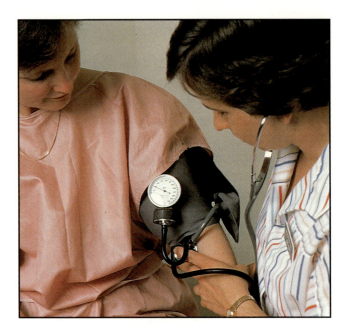

Blood pressure is regularly checked

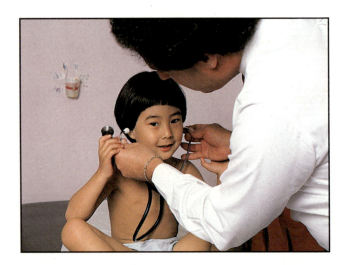

Clinics are a good way to meet other people with diabetes and also can be useful to learn about new ideas and treatments or discuss research that has appeared in the news.

On each visit, the doctors or nurses at the clinic should check blood glucose level, body weight, and look at blood or urine testing records. Also, injection sites and feet are often checked. Periodically, the eyes and kidneys are tested. These tests are especially important for those who have had the disorder for a long time.

Eye tests

If a person is diagnosed as having diabetes, their eyes should be checked every year or so. The test should include an examination of the blood vessels in the retina at the back of the eye. This is the part that receives the picture, like the film in a camera. If the blood vessels in the retina do become damaged, it can be treated using lasers. But, it is much better to try to prevent this condition occurring in the first place by having regular eye tests. In the first few weeks of diabetic treatment, blurred vision may occur as the glucose levels in the eye adjust. This usually clears in a week or two.

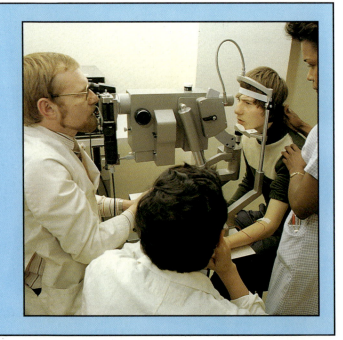

LEADING A NORMAL LIFE

People with diabetes live in a social world of family, friends and other relationships. These relationships are important in terms of practical and emotional support and may help a person with diabetes adjust to leading a normal and enjoyable life.

There is no reason why a healthy man or woman with diabetes should not have children. If a woman is going to have a baby there is no reason why she should not be able to care for the child until it is grown up, in the same way as other mothers who do not have diabetes. Once pregnancy is confirmed, however, a woman must maintain good control over diabetes. During the pregnancy it will probably be necessary to visit the clinic every 2 to 4 weeks so that diabetic control can be monitored as carefully as possible. The insulin requirement is likely to increase during pregnancy, especially during the second half.

Sport is for everybody. As exercise decreases the blood glucose levels and reduces the need for insulin, taking up a sport as a hobby is important for us all, but especially for people with diabetes.

Diabetic "Activity" camps provide an ideal opportunity for people with diabetes to try out a variety of different sports and activities, such as canoeing, skiing and sailing.

Specially trained staff also teach the children how to cope with tests, injections, "hypos" and the routine of daily living with diabetes. This helps children with diabetes to learn how to look after themselves and become more independent. Children can enjoy a holiday in a situation where they are the same as everyone else.

TAKING CARE OF YOUR BODY

High blood glucose levels can be harmful to long-term health. The best way to prevent health problems later in life is to keep diabetes under good control. This means behaving in a sensible manner and eating a balanced diet, not becoming overweight and taking regular exercise.

One problem is that most people with diabetes cannot "feel" when their diabetes is well controlled. So, it is very important for the blood glucose level to be constantly monitored and checked, with blood and urine tests. Very poor control leads to weight loss and more infections. Sometimes, but rarely, women with diabetes can have problems with their periods.

Stress, in the long run, has adverse affects on all of us – even those without diabetes – because of the hormones it produces and the extra strain on the heart. But, emotions have a direct effect on blood glucose levels and so diabetics need to be particularly aware of the effects of emotional upsets.

Healthy eating

A healthy diet should reduce refined sugar – except during illness and "hypos" for those with diabetes. The diet should include plenty of high fibre carbohydrate foods, such as wholemeal bread, beans and potatoes. These foods take longer to digest than do sweet foods, so that the glucose they contain is absorbed more slowly. This gives injected insulin time to work. Diabetes can upset the fat chemistry inside the body, so healthy eating also means cutting down on fatty foods such as butter, cream and meat fat.

Proteins are an essential part of a healthy diet, especially if the person with diabetes is still growing.

Becoming overweight can be harmful.

Foot care

People who have had diabetes for a long time – for 25 years or more – are prone to nerve damage, particularly in the legs and feet. The nerves are damaged due to excessive sugar and sugar products. This means that people with diabetes are particularly sensitive to foot injuries and infections. Diabetics should check their feet every day and wash and dry them properly. If there are any sore patches or fungal infections, a doctor should be consulted. Always wear comfortable shoes and never go barefoot.

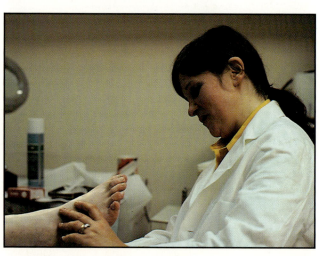
Feet should be checked regularly.

A healthy lifestyle

A healthy lifestyle helps to keep diabetes under control. Regular exercise and a healthy diet are important for everyone, but particularly for those with diabetes.

Children with diabetes can be immunized against childhood infections such as mumps, measles and German measles in the normal way. Infections cause difficulties with blood glucose control and this may occasionally delay healing of cuts and scratches. Diabetes is a unique disorder because, more than in any other illness, the patient has the responsibility of looking after themselves.

Foot care for a person with diabetes is important. Like everyone, they should wear comfortable shoes that fit well, and be careful when walking barefoot. Commonsense and hygiene are important. Toe nails should be cut straight across and not cut too short. Nobody, those with diabetes included, should smoke or drink too much alcohol. Alcohol contains calories so it tends to make people put on weight. It also blocks the release of glucose from the liver, and as a result, heavy drinking occasionally causes those with diabetes to have bad "hypos".

Cycling is a pleasurable hobby for all the family

A relaxed family holiday

Looking into the future

Much research is going on to try to find better forms of treatment for diabetes. Researchers have tried using drugs to suppress the immune system and to stop the body destroying islet cells. But these drugs do have side-effects, and it is hard to know for how long treatment would have to continue.

Other research workers have tried to alter the insulin molecule so that the insulin works much more quickly or much more slowly. These "designer insulins" show much promise.

Infusion pumps that feed insulin directly into the body to provide a small, continuous flow of insulin day and night, may help some people who find it difficult to control their diabetes. But infusion pumps are cumbersome and they need to be developed and refined before they can be used successfully.

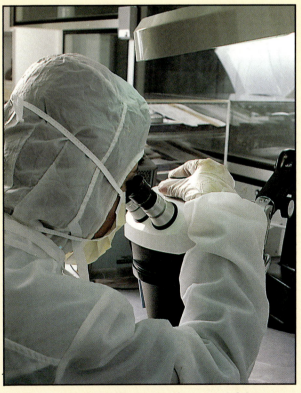
A "clean-room" in a bio-medical research laboratory

FIRST AID

It helps if friends, relatives, teachers or workmates learn how to recognize the symptoms of a "hypo" (see page 10) and know what to do. It is rare for anyone to be harmed by a "hypo". Even if a "hypo" is not treated, the body will usually increase the level of glucose in the blood and bring it back to normal. When driving a car, operating machinery or taking part in a "risky" sport, "hypo" can be dangerous.

To treat a "hypo", stop what the person is doing and give him or her something sweet to eat. Glucose tablets or drinks, or sugar lumps work quickly.

Most people on insulin carry a special card or wear a locket or bracelet that says they have diabetes and explains about treatment.

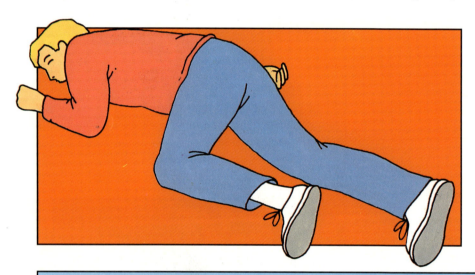

If anyone becomes unconscious, he or she should be turned on their side, and somebody should make sure that their airway is clear. First aid training teaches "ABC": Airways, Breathing, Circulation and this is a useful reminder of what to do.

If a person has a bad "hypo" a glucagon injection can be given.

People to contact

British Diabetic Association (BDA)
10 Queen Anne Street, London W1M 0BD. Tel 01-323-1531
The organization offers practical help and advice to all with diabetes. It produces a wide range of literature, videos and posters and organizes educational and activity holidays for all age groups. One of the major functions of the BDA is to support research into diabetes and promote proper treatments.

Medic-Alert Foundation
11/13 Clifton Terrace, London N4 3JP. Tel: 01-263-8596.

SOS Talisman
21 Grays Corner, Ley Street, Ilford, Essex IG2 7RQ.

The American Diabetes Association
National Service Center, 1660 Duke Street, Alexandra, VA 22314.

Juvenile Diabetes Foundation
60 Madison Avenue, New York, NY 10010.

67 Lawrence Road, London N15 4EY. Tel 01-809-7126

The Canadian Diabetes Association
78 Bond Street, Toronto, Ontario, M5B 2JB.

GLOSSARY

Acetone A sweet smelling ketone that may be smelt on the breath of people with ketones in the blood.

Acidosis A condition in which acids, usually derived from ketone, build up in the blood.

Adrenaline A hormone released in the body in response to a stress or emergency. For example, a fright, an illness or a hypoglycaemic reaction.

Alpha cells Cells in the islets of Langerhans in the pancreas that produce glucagon.

Beta cells Cells in the islets of Langerhans in the pancreas that produce insulin.

Calorie Unit used to measure the energy value of food.

Carbohydrates Foods that are digested in the intestine to produce simple sugars, such as glucose. Foods that contain carbohydrate include cakes, biscuits, bread, rice, pasta, oats and beans.

Coma A state of deep unconsciousness. In diabetes, it may be caused by severe hypoglycaemia or severe keto-acidosis.

Diet The variety of foods a person eats. A healthy diet is very important in controlling diabetes.

Glucagon A hormone produced in the islets of Langerhans cells of the pancreas, which raises the level of glucose in the blood.

Glucose A simple sugar obtained from the carbohydrates in food. Glucose is one of the main sources of energy for the body.

Glycogen The form in which glucose is stored in the liver and muscles.

Hormones Substances made in the body by endocrine glands. Hormones move around the body in the bloodstream and control vital body processes such as growth, digestion and blood glucose levels. Insulin is a hormone.

Hyperglycaemia A high blood glucose level.

Hypoglycaemia or "hypo" A low blood glucose level.

Insulin A hormone produced in the islets of Langerhans in the pancreas. It helps glucose penetrate the body cells where glucose is either used or stored, and so lowers blood glucose levels.

Islets of Langerhans Groups of cells in the pancreas. One type of islet cell produces insulin.

Ketoacidosis, or ketosis Hyperglucaemias A build-up of ketones in the body which leads to acidosis.

Ketones Substances produced when fats are broken down. They smell of acetone (nail varnish remover) and make the blood acidic.

Pancreas Large gland in the abdomen, which produces digestive juices and the hormones insulin and glucagon.

Renal threshold Blood glucose level above which glucose spills over into the urine.

Retina Layer of light-sensitive cells at the back of the eye.

Retinopathy Damage to the retina which may be caused by long-term diabetes, and in extreme cases, might lead to blindness.

INDEX

Adrenaline 10, 21
Alcohol 29
Alpha cells 5
American Diabetic
  Association 12

Banting, Frederick 13
Best, Charles 13
Beta cell 5, 8, 18
Bile duct 4
Blurred vision 26
British Diabetic Association
  12

Calorie 29
Carbohydrates 4, 15
Chiropodist 26
Clinic 20, 22, 23, 26, 27
Collip 13
Controlled diet 9
Convulsions 10

Delta cells 5
Designer insulin 29
Diabetes mellitus 4
Diabetic Activity Camps 27
Diabetic Associations 23
Diabetic cycle 7
Diabetic diet 15
Diabetic food 15
Diet 15, 29
Digestive juices 5, 13
Driving 24

Exercise 10, 15, 25, 27, 28, 29
Eye disease 11
Eye tests 26

Fats 7, 15, 22

Food 15, 28
Foot care 28, 29
Foot problems 11
Future treatments 29

Glucagon 4, 5, 6
Glucose 6, 7, 10, 16, 17, 18,
  20, 21, 22, 27, 28, 29
  glucose control 15
  glucose level 26
Glycogen 6

High Commission 25
High-fibre 15
Hormones 21, 28
Human insulin 18
Hyperglycaemia 7
Hypoglycaemia 10, 15, 16,
  21, 23, 24, 25, 28, 29

Immunization 29
Injections 21, 27
Insulin 4, 5, 7, 8, 10, 13, 15,
  17, 18, 19, 22, 25, 28
  discovery of 8
  fast-acting 13, 17
  long-acting 17
  maintaining the level 14
  slow-acting 13
  soluble 13
Insulin molecule 29
Insulin-dependent diabetes
  8, 9, 13, 7, 24
Islets of Langerhans 4, 5, 6, 29

Juvenile onset diabetes 9

Ketoacidosis 7, 8
Ketones 7, 8

Ketosis 7

Langerhans 5
Lectin 18
Lifestyle 20, 29
Liver 5, 6, 29

Macleod 13
Maturity onset diabetes 9

Non-insulin-dependent
  diabetes (NIDDM) 8, 9,
  15, 25, 28

Oesophagus 5

Pancreas 4, 5, 17
Pancreatic duct 4
Pancreatic extract 13
Pen therapy 17
Pregnancy 27
Proteins 7, 13, 15

Retina 11, 26

Smoking 29
Sport 20, 23, 27, 29
Stomach 5
Stress 22, 28

Tablets 15, 16, 25
Thompson, Leonard 13
Time zones 25
Type I diabetes 9
Type II diabetes 9

Urine 7, 8, 12
Urine tests 11, 14

Weight loss 8, 15

Photographic Credits:
Cover and pages 14 both, 27t and 28b: British Diabetic Association; pages 5t, 11t, 11m and 26b: Biophoto Associates; pages 5b, 9t, 9m, 11tm, 11b, 12 both, 13, 19m, 19b, 21, 26t and 26m: Science Photo Library; pages 8 all, 15, 16 all, 20 both, 22b, 23, 25t and 29t: Roger Vlitos; pages 9, 23m, 25b, 28t and 29b: J. Allan Cash Photo Library; page 17: Novo Labs; page 19t: Royal Victoria Hospital, Belfast; pages 22t, 24 all and 27tl: Zefa; page 23t: Robert Harding Library; pages 23b, 25m, 27b and 29m: Images/Biophoto Associates.